W9-DCU-172

Sports Illustrated KIDS

STARS OF SPORTS

MALLORY PUGH

SOCCER SUPERSTAR

■■❚❚ by Shane Frederick

CAPSTONE PRESS
a capstone imprint

Stars of Sports is published by Capstone Press, an imprint of Capstone.
1710 Roe Crest Drive, North Mankato, Minnesota 56003
www.capstonepub.com

**Library of Congress Cataloging-in-Publication Data is available on the Library of
Congress website.**
ISBN: 978-1-4966-8380-9 (library binding)
ISBN: 978-1-4966-8431-8 (eBook PDF)

Summary: As a child, Mallory Pugh would do anything she could to watch soccer, practice
soccer, and play soccer. She was soccer obsessed! Not much has changed for Pugh in
terms of her passion for soccer. Learn about Pugh's highlights on the field in this thrilling
biography in the Stars of Sports series.

Editorial Credits
Editor: Anna Butzer; Designer: Sarah Bennett; Media Researcher: Eric Gohl; Production
Specialist: Laura Manthe

Image Credits
Associated Press: The Canadian Press/Jason Franson, 12; Getty Images: AAron Ontiveroz,
11, FIFA/Ian Walton, 20, FIFA/Matthew Lewis, 21, Hyoung Chang, 14, Karl Gehring, 9,
Stringer/Bruno Zanardo, 19; iStockphoto: milehightraveler, 6; Newscom: Icon Sportswire/
Robin Alam, cover, Icon Sportswire/Scott Winters, 17, 23, 25, Sipa USA/Abaca Press/Eliot
Blondet, 27, ZUMA Press/Bryan Byerly, 7, ZUMA Press/Mark Smith, 5, ZUMA Press/Vi-
Images/Gerrit Van Keulen, 28; Shutterstock: winui, 1

Direct Quotations
Page 7, "It was 2v1 and . . ." USA Soccer, "Mallory Pugh," https://www.ussoccer.com/
players/p/mallory-pugh
Accessed on March 18, 2020.

Page 8, "I remember at U-11 . . ." Noah Davis, "The Next Great American Soccer Star?"
August 2, 2016, https://www.newyorker.com/sports/sporting-scene/the-next-great-
american-soccer-star
Accessed on March 18, 2020.

Page 16, "I'd seen Mal in . . ." MHS Staff, "Meteoric rise: Colorado native Mallory Pugh gets
to make a splash on a global stage," June 11, 2019, https://milehighsports.com/meteoric-
rise-colorado-native-mallory-pugh-gets-set-to-make-a-splash-on-a-global-stage/
Accessed on March 18, 2020.

Page 18, "I don't pay any attention . . ." J Moninger, "On Goal with Mallory Pugh,"
September 23, 2017, https://healthwellnesscolorado.com/on-goal-with-mallory-pugh/
Accessed on March 18, 2020.

Page 27, "After the final, . . ." FIFA, "World Cup debut inspires Pugh to strive for
greatness," September 12, 2019, https://www.fifa.com/womensworldcup/news/world-cup-
debut-inspires-pugh-to-strive-for-greatness
Accessed on March 18, 2020.

All internet sites appearing in back matter were available and accurate when this book was
sent to press.

TABLE OF CONTENTS

Glossary terms are **BOLD** on first use.

FUTURE STAR

Mallory Pugh stayed **onside** as the soccer ball rolled through the defense. She found a burst of speed and ran ahead with the ball. The goalkeeper slid down to try to stop her, but Pugh made a move and got around her. The net was left wide open, and she kicked the ball in for a goal.

It was the 11th goal in the United States' 13–0 win over Thailand. It was a special score for Pugh. It was her first World Cup goal. The first player to celebrate with her was teammate Megan Rapinoe. The 34-year-old Rapinoe would be the star of the 2019 FIFA Women's World Cup, leading the U.S. to a championship. But 21-year-old Mallory Pugh **represented** what was to come in U.S. women's soccer.

Pugh breaks past Thailand's goalkeeper to score a goal during the Women's World Cup in 2019.

〉〉〉

CHAPTER ONE

LOVE OF THE GAME

Mallory Pugh was born on April 29, 1998, in Littleton, Colorado. She grew up in the town of Highlands Ranch, Colorado. She loved two things more than anything—soccer and her older sister, Brianna.

〈〈〈 Pugh's hometown of Highlands Ranch is just south of Denver (shown).

>>> Mallory poses with her family at Rio
Tinto Stadium in Utah. She and her sister,
Brianna (top left), were close growing up.

Brianna and her friends played soccer in the
backyard. Mallory would try to play with them. The
older girls didn't take it easy on young Mal. They
passed the ball around her and made her work hard to
get it. "It was 2v1 and I was five years younger," Pugh
said. "It was so unfair. But it was so good for me."

FOLLOWING HER BIG SISTER

Mallory went to all of her big sister's soccer games. When she could, Mallory would sit on the bench with Brianna's team. Mallory started playing organized soccer too. The backyard games with Brianna helped make Mallory one of the best players her age in the state. Her speed and footwork impressed coaches, teammates, and opponents.

"I remember at U-11 thinking that she's the most **impactful** player I've ever coached," one coach said. "That didn't mean she was the best player I had ever coached at that age, but she had the biggest impact in the game, the biggest impact in training."

>>> Brianna Pugh played soccer at Mountain
Vista High School and at the University
of Oregon. She helped build her younger
sister's soccer skills.

Mallory Pugh also had a big impact on the teams she played for. In 2010 and 2011, she led her team, Real Colorado, to back-to-back state championships. Coaches at the national level were starting to notice. They invited her to participate in national camps. The camps took Mallory all over the country.

A couple years later, Mallory started playing soccer all around the world. At the age of 15, she earned a spot on the U.S. Under-17 National Team. She went to Jamaica for the U-17 World Championships in 2013. With five goals and three **assists**, she led the team in scoring. Her team took third place.

>>> Pugh shows her athleticism while posing for a photo at her family home in 2011.

A RISING YOUNG STAR

In 2014, Pugh started the year with the United States U-17 team. Later that year, she got called up to the U-20 team. She played in the U-20 Women's World Cup in Canada. She was the youngest player on the team. The next season, Pugh was one of the country's best U-20 players.

》》》 Pugh (left) races toward the ball ahead of Brazil's Julia Bianchi in a U-20 World Cup game in Alberta, Canada, in 2014.

Pugh and the U.S. team traveled to Honduras in 2015. There they played for the Confederation of North, Central America, and Caribbean Association Football U-20 Championship. This tournament would determine the best women's soccer team at that age level in North America. It would also determine who would play in the next U-20 World Cup. Pugh was the U.S. captain, and she led Team USA to a tournament title. She was the top scorer in the tournament with seven goals. She won the title of Most Valuable Player (MVP) for the tournament.

FACT

In 2015, Pugh was named Gatorade National Girls Soccer Player of the Year. She was also named Youth Girls National Player of the Year by the National Soccer Coaches Association of America.

THE NEXT BIG THING

While she was playing for the national teams, Pugh was also playing for her high school team back in Colorado. She was hard to stop on the **pitch**.

As a ninth-grader, Pugh scored 10 goals in 14 games and led Mountain Vista to the Colorado state championship. The next season, she scored 13 goals, even though she played in just eight games because of her national team commitments. Her junior season was her best season at Mountain Vista. Pugh dominated, scoring 24 goals in 10 games. That's an average of 2.4 goals per game. In three seasons with Mountain Vista, Pugh scored 47 goals. She assisted on 21 others in just 32 games.

Some people called her the "next big thing" for American soccer. They have even compared her to the great Mia Hamm.

⟨⟨⟨ Pugh was a star of the Mountain Vista
High School soccer team.

CHAPTER THREE

PLAYING WITH THE BEST

Pugh's performance in Honduras caught the attention of U.S. women's soccer coach Jill Ellis. Even though Pugh was just 17, it was time to call her up to the big club. "I'd seen Mal in our youth national teams and knew she was special," Ellis said.

On January 23, 2016, Pugh made her **debut** with the U.S. national team. The team was playing a friendly game against Ireland. Pugh was the youngest player to play for Team USA in 11 years. But she proved that she fit right in with the country's best players when she headed a ball into the net for her first goal.

>>> Pugh remains airborne after making a header in a match with Costa Rica in July 2016. She scored her third goal for Team USA during the match.

TO THE OLYMPICS

Not long after making her debut with the U.S. team, Pugh was picked to go to the Olympics in 2016. Once again, Pugh was the youngest player on the team, but that didn't seem to matter. When she scored in a game against Colombia, Pugh was the youngest U.S. soccer player to score a goal in the Olympics.

"I don't pay any attention to the hype surrounding my age," she said. "As people like to say, age is just a number."

FACT

Pugh was the second-youngest U.S. soccer player ever to compete in the Olympics. Only Cindy Parlow, in 1996, was younger, by a month.

>>> Pugh fights for the ball in a match against
Colombia during the 2016 Olympic Games.

ANOTHER WORLD CUP

Pugh graduated from Mountain Vista High School in the spring of 2016. Graduation was followed by the Olympics. Then she had a chance to play in another U-20 World Cup. Pugh was named team captain.

〉〉〉 Pugh controls the balls in the quarterfinal match against Mexico in the 2016 U-20 World Cup.

>>> Pugh celebrates after scoring her goal in the 2016 U-20 World Cup.

The U.S. team traveled to Papua New Guinea for the tournament and took fourth place. Pugh scored two goals in the tournament. The U.S. lost 1–0 to Japan in the third-place match.

Super Fan

Because of her commitment to the U.S. team, Pugh couldn't play for her high school team as a senior. But Pugh still wanted to support her teammates as much as possible. She continued to practice with them and cheer for them from the sidelines.

CHAPTER FOUR

TURNING PRO

Pugh decided while she was in high school to go to the University of California–Los Angeles (UCLA). She would study there and play soccer. Mallory put off going to UCLA for one semester to play in the U-20 World Cup. After arriving at UCLA, she joined the soccer team. She played three spring games for the Bruins.

After the spring semester ended, Pugh had a very tough decision to make. Even though many top players came through college soccer, she wondered if it was right for her. She decided to leave college to play **professional** soccer. Soon she signed a contract with the Washington Spirit of the National Women's Soccer League (NWSL).

〉〉〉 Pugh joined the Washington Spirit in May 2017.

PRO DEBUT

Pugh was just 18 years old when she decided to turn pro. No American woman had ever skipped college to join the NWSL. Pugh was now living on her own instead of with friends in college.

Pugh said she didn't want to be comfortable. She wanted to be challenged in life and in soccer. She believes that people often grow from dealing with the big, uncomfortable moments in life.

Pugh made her debut with the Spirit on May 20, 2017. She scored her first goal on June 3 against the Houston Dash. She was the youngest NWSL player ever to score a goal. Pugh finished that first season with six goals. She led the Spirit in scoring. She was named Washington's most valuable player. She was also a finalist for league rookie of the year.

〉〉〉 Even in her first pro season, defenders had a hard time stopping Pugh.

A League of Their Own

The National Women's Soccer League is the top professional league in the United States. There are nine teams. Besides the Washington Spirit, the league includes the Chicago Red Stars, Houston Dash, OL Reign, Sky Blue FC, Portland Thorns FC, Utah Royals FC, Orlando Pride, and North Carolina Courage.

U.S. WORLD CUP WIN

In 2018, Pugh scored just two goals and assisted on another for the Spirit. She missed two months of playing because of a knee injury. But she still played in 15 games. In 2019, she played in just nine games because she went to France with the U.S. national team. She would play in the Women's World Cup.

At 21 years old, Pugh was the second-youngest player on the U.S. team at the World Cup. She played in three of her team's seven games. The older players led the way to a thrilling championship. The U.S. defeated Netherlands 2–0 in the final game.

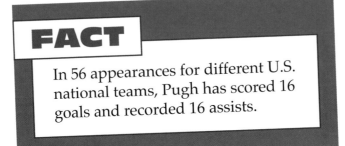

FACT

In 56 appearances for different U.S. national teams, Pugh has scored 16 goals and recorded 16 assists.

Pugh dashes toward the ball in a Women's ⟩⟩⟩
World Cup match against Chile in 2019.

"After the final, I felt like I've never been so motivated in my life," Pugh said. "I've never felt anything like that—it's the best feeling ever, and I want to feel that again. I now know the work required to put in, but I also know there's so much more that has to happen. I just have to keep pushing."

MORE TO COME

Pugh scored only one goal against Thailand and did not get much playing time during the 2019 World Cup. But she learned a lot from the team's star forwards. Megan Rapinoe, Alex Morgan, and Carli Lloyd set great examples. They became celebrities that summer.

The next World Cup is in 2023. Pugh is already a star soccer player. But that year, it will be her turn to lead the U.S. team on the world stage.

》》》 Pugh and teammate Lindsey Horan pose for a photo at the 2019 Women's World Cup.

TIMELINE

1998 Born in Littleton, Colorado

2011 Leads the Real Colorado team to the state championships for the second year in a row

2013 Begins playing soccer on the U.S. Under-17 National Team

2014 Begins playing for the U.S. U-20 team and is the youngest player on the team

2015 Named Youth Girls National Player of the Year

2016 Makes debut with the U.S. national team

2016 Plays for the Olympic team and becomes the youngest U.S. soccer player to score a goal in the Olympics

2017 Makes her professional debut on the Washington Spirit team with the National Women's Soccer League

2019 Plays in the Women's World Cup with the U.S. National Team

GLOSSARY

ASSIST (uh-SIST)—a pass that leads to a goal

DEBUT (DAY-byoo)—a first appearance

IMPACT (IM-pakt)—to have a strong effect

ONSIDE (on-SIDE)—in a position to legally receive a pass

PITCH (PICH)—an outdoor playing area for various sports

PROFESSIONAL (pruh-FESH-uh-nuhl)—a level of sports in which players get paid to play

REPRESENT (rep-ri-zent)—to be an example of

READ MORE

Cooley Peterson, Megan. *Soccer Rules!* North Mankato, MN: Black Rabbit Books, 2018.

Killion, Ann. *Champions of Women's Soccer.* New York: Philomel Books, 2018.

Williams, Heather. *Soccer: A Guide for Players and Fans.* North Mankato, MN: Capstone Press, 2020.

INTERNET SITES

FIFA
www.fifa.com

Team USA
www.teamusa.org

USA Soccer: Mallory Pugh
www.ussoccer.com/players/p/mallory-pugh

INDEX